About the author:

_____

_____

Contact info:

_____

NOVEL from NOTHING

* * *

The Ultimate Fiction Writer's Organizer

By Hannah Beilenson and Sarah Longstreth

PETER PAUPER PRESS, INC.
WHITE PLAINS, NEW YORK

PETER PAUPER PRESS
Fine Books and Gifts Since 1928

OUR COMPANY

In 1928, at the age of twenty-two, Peter Beilenson began printing books on a small press in the basement of his parents' home in Larchmont, New York. Peter—and later, his wife, Edna—sought to create fine books that sold at "prices even a pauper could afford."

Today, still family owned and operated, Peter Pauper Press continues to honor our founders' legacy—and our customers' expectations—of beauty, quality, and value.

———

For Matt and Roy, the world's best writing partners

— SL

For Serena, a great writer and friend
— HB

Special thanks to Oren Shoemaker

Cover designed by Heather Zschock
Interior design by Margaret Rubiano

Images used under license from Shutterstock.com

Published in the United Kingdom and Europe by
Peter Pauper Press, Inc. c/o White Pebble International
Units 2-3, Spring Business Park
Stanbridge Road
Havant, Hampshire PO9 2GJ, UK

7 6 5 4 3 2 1

Visit us at www.peterpauper.com

CONTENTS

Don't worry about imagination.
You have all the imagination you need,
and all the reading, journaling, writing,
and learning you will be doing will
stimulate it. Play with your ideas.
Have fun with them. Don't worry about
being silly or outrageous or wrong.
Persist.
— OCTAVIA BUTLER

* * *

WELCOME

If you're reading this, it's probably because you know you have a book inside you, waiting to come out. You have all it takes to make that happen, and the journal you're holding can help.

Use these pages to gather everything you need to write that book. Set goals, create your cast of characters, develop your setting, sketch the skeleton of your story, and start filling in the pieces. Interactive prompts will help you practice storytelling fundamentals and get your creative juices flowing.

Don't make it perfect. You have never read a book that sprang out from the author's brain full-grown and dressed in battle armor. First drafts are messy, so get messy! There'll always be time to revise.

When you're ready, sit down and write. Keep this journal with you to keep track of your ideas, give yourself an inspiration boost, and cheer yourself on as you progress. Even if you change things around from what you write in the pages that follow—you probably will—you'll prove to yourself that your imagination can make something vivid, visionary, and uniquely yours.

Everyone's story deserves to be told. It's time to conquer the blank page and bring yours to life.

You've got this!

GOALS CHECKLIST

Use the table below to track your writing goals. A daily (or weekly) word count can keep you motivated. Add a check mark every time you meet a goal, and give yourself a star when you exceed it!

Use the space below to keep tracking word count or add other goals you want to focus on.

GOAL	PROGRESS	FINISHED!
_400_ WORDS PER DAY	✓✓✓✓✓✓✓ *a week's worth of writing!*	☆
_____ WORDS PER DAY	○○○○○○○	
_____ WORDS PER DAY	○○○○○○○	
_____ WORDS PER DAY	○○○○○○○	
_____ WORDS PER DAY	○○○○○○○	
_____ WORDS PER DAY	○○○○○○○	
_____ WORDS PER DAY	○○○○○○○	
_____ WORDS PER DAY	○○○○○○○	
_____ WORDS PER DAY	○○○○○○○	
_____ WORDS PER DAY	○○○○○○○	
_____ WORDS PER DAY	○○○○○○○	
_____ WORDS PER DAY	○○○○○○○	
_____ WORDS PER DAY	○○○○○○○	
_____ WORDS PER DAY	○○○○○○○	

Don't worry if you miss a day—just keep trying. You can always adjust your goal depending on what you discover about your own pace.

GOAL	PROGRESS	FINISHED!
_____ WORDS PER DAY	○○○○○○○	
_____ WORDS PER DAY	○○○○○○○	
_____ WORDS PER DAY	○○○○○○○	
_____ WORDS PER DAY	○○○○○○○	
_____ WORDS PER DAY	○○○○○○○	
_____ WORDS PER DAY	○○○○○○○	
_____ WORDS PER DAY	○○○○○○○	
_____ WORDS PER DAY	○○○○○○○	
_____ WORDS PER DAY	○○○○○○○	
_____ WORDS PER DAY	○○○○○○○	
_____ WORDS PER DAY	○○○○○○○	
_____ WORDS PER DAY	○○○○○○○	
_____ WORDS PER DAY	○○○○○○○	
_____ WORDS PER DAY	○○○○○○○	
_____ WORDS PER DAY	○○○○○○○	

*I was further learning that
my characters would do my work
for me, if I let them alone, if I gave
them their heads, which is to say,
their fantasies, their frights.*
— RAY BRADBURY

***

CHARACTER CREATION

PROTAGONIST

Whether a hero of destiny or an ordinary person, your protagonist is the heart of your story. If you care about them and love what they love, your readers will love them too.

What they're called:

What they do:

Why I love them:

Why they're flawed:

What they want: ....

....

....

....

....

....

Why they can't have it (yet): ....

....

....

....

....

Add a drawing or photo below!

Appearance: ....

....

....

....

....

....

....

DEUTERAGONIST

If you have a second main character, give them some love too. (If you have more, let them take up extra space in the Cast of Characters section.)

What they're called:

What they do:

Why I love them:

Why they're flawed:

What they want: ....

....

....

....

....

....

Why they can't have it (yet): ....

....

....

....

....

....

Add a drawing or photo below!

Appearance: ....

....

....

....

....

....

ANTAGONIST

Alluring, sympathetic, redeemable, or simply horrible—whoever they are, they spell trouble.

What they're called:

_____

_____

_____

_____

Who they are to the protagonist/s:

_____

_____

_____

_____

What they want: _____

_____

_____

_____

_____

Why it causes conflict: _____

_____

_____

_____

_____

_____

Why they're awful: ....

....

....

....

....

....

....

Why they kind of have a point (optional—pure evil villains are always in style):

....

....

....

....

....

Add a drawing or photo below!

Appearance: ....

....

....

....

....

....

....

CAST OF CHARACTERS

Use these pages to get to know your characters—how they look, move, and speak; what they want; how they love.

NAME: ....

Appearance: ....

Relationships: ....

Hopes: ....

....

....

Fears: ....

....

....

Wants: ....

....

....

Problems: ....

....

....

....

What makes them unique? ....

....

....

....

NAME: ....

Appearance: ....

Relationships: ....

Hopes: ....

....

....

....

Fears: ....

....

....

....

Wants: ....

....

....

Problems: ....

....

....

....

What makes them unique? ....

....

....

....

CAST OF CHARACTERS

NAME: ....

Appearance: ....

Relationships: ....

Hopes: ....

....

....

....

Fears: ....

....

....

Wants: ....

....

....

Problems: ....

....

....

....

What makes them unique? ....

....

....

....

NAME: ....

Appearance: ....

Relationships: ....

Hopes: ....

....

....

....

Fears: ....

....

....

....

Wants: ....

....

....

Problems: ....

....

....

....

What makes them unique? ....

....

....

....

CAST OF CHARACTERS

NAME: ....

Appearance: ....

Relationships: ....

Hopes: ....

....

....

....

Fears: ....

....

....

Wants: ....

....

....

Problems: ....

....

....

....

What makes them unique? ....

....

....

....

NAME: ....

Appearance: ....

Relationships: ....

Hopes: ....

....

....

....

Fears: ....

....

....

....

Wants: ....

....

....

Problems: ....

....

....

....

What makes them unique? ....

....

....

....

CAST OF CHARACTERS

NAME: ....

Appearance: ....

Relationships: ....

Hopes: ....

....

....

....

Fears: ....

....

....

Wants: ....

....

....

Problems: ....

....

....

What makes them unique? ....

....

....

....

NAME: ....

Appearance: ....

Relationships: ....

Hopes: ....

....

....

....

Fears: ....

....

....

....

Wants: ....

....

....

Problems: ....

....

....

....

What makes them unique? ....

....

....

....

CAST OF CHARACTERS

NAME: ....

Appearance: ....

Relationships: ....

Hopes: ....

....

....

....

Fears: ....

....

....

Wants: ....

....

....

Problems: ....

....

....

....

What makes them unique? ....

....

....

....

NAME: ....

Appearance: ....

Relationships: ....

Hopes: ....

....

....

....

Fears: ....

....

....

....

Wants: ....

....

....

Problems: ....

....

....

....

What makes them unique? ....

....

....

....

CAST OF CHARACTERS

NAME: ....

Appearance: ....

Relationships: ....

Hopes: ....

....

....

....

Fears: ....

....

....

Wants: ....

....

....

Problems: ....

....

....

....

What makes them unique? ....

....

....

....

NAME: ....

Appearance: ....

Relationships: ....

Hopes: ....

....

....

....

Fears: ....

....

....

....

Wants: ....

....

....

Problems: ....

....

....

....

What makes them unique? ....

....

....

....

CAST OF CHARACTERS

NAME: ....

Appearance: ....

Relationships: ....

Hopes: ....

....

....

....

Fears: ....

....

....

Wants: ....

....

....

Problems: ....

....

....

....

What makes them unique? ....

....

....

....

NAME: ....

Appearance: ....

Relationships: ....

Hopes: ....

....

....

....

Fears: ....

....

....

....

Wants: ....

....

....

Problems: ....

....

....

....

What makes them unique? ....

....

....

....

CAST OF CHARACTERS

NAME: ....

Appearance: ....

Relationships: ....

Hopes: ....

....

....

....

Fears: ....

....

....

Wants: ....

....

....

Problems: ....

....

....

....

What makes them unique? ....

....

....

....

NAME: ....

Appearance: ....

Relationships: ....

Hopes: ....

....

....

....

Fears: ....

....

....

....

Wants: ....

....

....

Problems: ....

....

....

....

What makes them unique? ....

....

....

....

CAST OF CHARACTERS

NAME: ....

Appearance: ....

Relationships: ....

Hopes: ....

....

....

....

Fears: ....

....

....

Wants: ....

....

....

Problems: ....

....

....

....

What makes them unique? ....

....

....

....

NAME: ....

Appearance: ....

Relationships: ....

Hopes: ....

....

....

....

Fears: ....

....

....

....

Wants: ....

....

....

Problems: ....

....

....

....

What makes them unique? ....

....

....

....

CAST OF CHARACTERS

NAME: ....

Appearance: ....

Relationships: ....

Hopes: ....

....

....

....

Fears: ....

....

....

Wants: ....

....

....

Problems: ....

....

....

....

What makes them unique? ....

....

....

....

NAME: ....

Appearance: ....

Relationships: ....

Hopes: ....

....

....

....

Fears: ....

....

....

....

Wants: ....

....

....

Problems: ....

....

....

....

What makes them unique? ....

....

....

....

RELATIONSHIP MAP

Character maps can help you document all of the relationships in your story. The map is a reference to keep in mind as you write scenes with these characters in them. Here's one example.

THE GREAT GATSBY

friends

in love with

friends

???

cousins

kills

Jay Gatsby
Wealthy Businessman

Nick Carraway
New York Newcomer

Daisy Buchanan
Beautiful Socialite

George Wilson
Auto Shop Owner

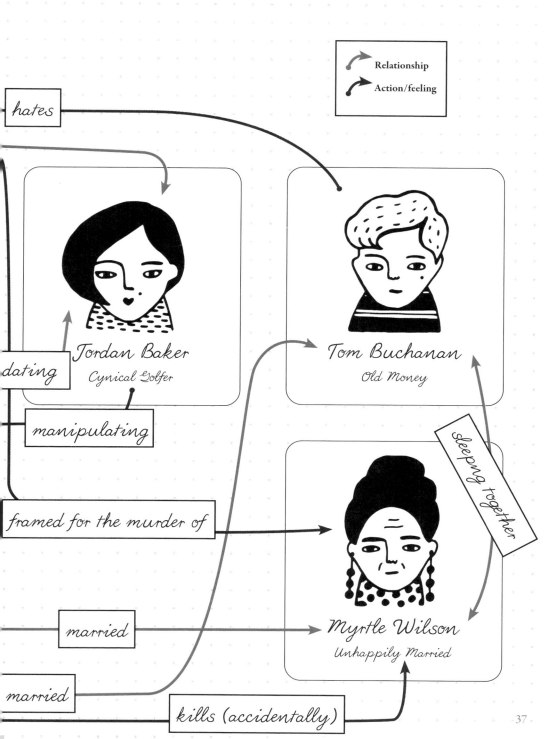

Relationship

Action/feeling

hates

Jordan Baker
Cynical Golfer

Tom Buchanan
Old Money

dating

manipulating

sleeping together

framed for the murder of

Myrtle Wilson
Unhappily Married

married

married

kills (accidentally)

37

RELATIONSHIP MAP

Your turn! Use the space below to map your characters' relationships. Draw new boxes and lines as needed.

Name:

Role:

Name:

Role:

Name:

Role:

Name:

Role:

Name:

Role:

Name:

Role:

Name:

Role:

Name:

Role:

*One writes a story to find out what
happens in it. Before it is written it sits in
the mind like a piece of overheard gossip. . . .
The story process is like taking up such a piece
of gossip, hunting down the people
actually involved, questioning them,
finding out what really occurred, and
visiting pertinent locations.*
— SAMUEL DELANY

* * *

SETTING

YOUR WORLD

What's the mood of your story? How can your overall setting help create that tone?

_____

_____

_____

_____

What do you need your reader to know about your world?

_____

_____

_____

_____

_____

_____

Overall setting: *(dinky suburb? fractured empire?)*

_____

_____

_____

_____

Who lives here?

_____

_____

Who's got power?

Features: *(food? climate? landmarks?)*

If you traveled here, what would you remember?

If this was your home, what would you miss about it when you left?

IMPORTANT PLACES

PLACE: ....

Significance: ....

....

Landmarks: ....

....

....

Sights, sounds, smells: ....

....

....

How it feels to be here: ....

....

....

....

People you can find here: ....

....

....

....

PLACE: ....

Significance: ....

....

Landmarks: ....

....

....

....

Sights, sounds, smells: ....

....

....

....

How it feels to be here: ....

....

....

....

....

People you can find here: ....

....

....

....

....

IMPORTANT PLACES

PLACE: ....

Significance: ....

....

Landmarks: ....

....

....

Sights, sounds, smells: ....

....

....

How it feels to be here: ....

....

....

....

....

People you can find here: ....

....

....

....

PLACE: ....

Significance: ....

....

Landmarks: ....

....

....

....

Sights, sounds, smells: ....

....

....

....

How it feels to be here: ....

....

....

....

....

People you can find here: ....

....

....

....

....

IMPORTANT PLACES

PLACE: ....

Significance: ....

....

Landmarks: ....

....

....

....

Sights, sounds, smells: ....

....

....

....

How it feels to be here: ....

....

....

....

....

People you can find here: ....

....

....

....

PLACE: ....

Significance: ....

....

Landmarks: ....

....

....

....

Sights, sounds, smells: ....

....

....

....

How it feels to be here: ....

....

....

....

....

People you can find here: ....

....

....

....

IMPORTANT PLACES

PLACE: ....

Significance: ....

....

Landmarks: ....

....

....

....

Sights, sounds, smells: ....

....

....

....

How it feels to be here: ....

....

....

....

....

....

People you can find here: ....

....

....

....

....

PLACE: ....

Significance: ....

....

Landmarks: ....

....

....

....

Sights, sounds, smells: ....

....

....

....

How it feels to be here: ....

....

....

....

....

People you can find here: ....

....

....

....

....

IMPORTANT PLACES

PLACE: ....

Significance: ....

....

Landmarks: ....

....

....

....

Sights, sounds, smells: ....

....

....

....

How it feels to be here: ....

....

....

....

....

People you can find here: ....

....

....

....

PLACE: ....

Significance: ....

....

Landmarks: ....

....

....

....

Sights, sounds, smells: ....

....

....

....

How it feels to be here: ....

....

....

....

....

People you can find here: ....

....

....

....

IMPORTANT PLACES

PLACE: ....

Significance: ....

....

Landmarks: ....

....

....

....

Sights, sounds, smells: ....

....

....

....

How it feels to be here: ....

....

....

....

....

People you can find here: ....

....

....

....

PLACE: ....

Significance: ....

....

Landmarks: ....

....

....

....

Sights, sounds, smells: ....

....

....

....

How it feels to be here: ....

....

....

....

....

People you can find here: ....

....

....

....

....

IMPORTANT PLACES

PLACE: ....

Significance: ....

....

Landmarks: ....

....

....

....

Sights, sounds, smells: ....

....

....

....

How it feels to be here: ....

....

....

....

....

People you can find here: ....

....

....

....

PLACE: ....

Significance: ....

....

Landmarks: ....

....

....

....

Sights, sounds, smells: ....

....

....

....

How it feels to be here: ....

....

....

....

....

People you can find here: ....

....

....

....

....

IMPORTANT PLACES

PLACE: ....

Significance: ....

....

Landmarks: ....

....

....

Sights, sounds, smells: ....

....

....

How it feels to be here: ....

....

....

....

....

People you can find here: ....

....

....

....

PLACE: ....

Significance: ....

....

Landmarks: ....

....

....

....

Sights, sounds, smells: ....

....

....

....

How it feels to be here: ....

....

....

....

....

People you can find here: ....

....

....

....

....

IMPORTANT PLACES

PLACE: ....

Significance: ....

....

Landmarks: ....

....

....

....

Sights, sounds, smells: ....

....

....

....

How it feels to be here: ....

....

....

....

....

People you can find here: ....

....

....

....

PLACE: ....

Significance: ....

....

Landmarks: ....

....

....

....

Sights, sounds, smells: ....

....

....

....

How it feels to be here: ....

....

....

....

....

People you can find here: ....

....

....

....

....

IMPORTANT PLACES

PLACE: ....

Significance: ....

....

Landmarks: ....

....

....

....

Sights, sounds, smells: ....

....

....

....

How it feels to be here: ....

....

....

....

....

People you can find here: ....

....

....

....

....

PLACE: ....

Significance: ....

....

Landmarks: ....

....

....

....

Sights, sounds, smells: ....

....

....

....

How it feels to be here: ....

....

....

....

....

People you can find here: ....

....

....

....

IMPORTANT PLACES

PLACE: ....

Significance: ....

....

Landmarks: ....

....

....

....

Sights, sounds, smells: ....

....

....

....

How it feels to be here: ....

....

....

....

....

People you can find here: ....

....

....

....

PLACE: ....

Significance: ....

....

Landmarks: ....

....

....

....

Sights, sounds, smells: ....

....

....

....

How it feels to be here: ....

....

....

....

....

People you can find here: ....

....

....

....

....

IMPORTANT PLACES

PLACE: ....

Significance: ....

....

Landmarks: ....

....

....

....

Sights, sounds, smells: ....

....

....

....

How it feels to be here: ....

....

....

....

....

People you can find here: ....

....

....

....

....

PLACE: ....

Significance: ....

....

Landmarks: ....

....

....

....

Sights, sounds, smells: ....

....

....

....

How it feels to be here: ....

....

....

....

....

People you can find here: ....

....

....

....

....

MAPS

Here's some space to visualize your setting. For those who aren't master cartographers, try something easy: draw a rectangle and you have a building; a few squares together and you have a neighborhood; a few lines and you have a river or a thoroughfare. If you're using a real place, you can tape a map into these pages.

Make [the] characters want something right away—even if it's only a glass of water. Characters paralyzed by the meaninglessness of modern life still have to drink water from time to time.
— KURT VONNEGUT

* * *

PLOT

STORY SPINE

Once upon a time there was . . .
Sum up your hero in one sentence.

_____

_____

_____

Every day . . .
Describe your world as it starts out, and what your characters do there.

_____

_____

_____

_____

_____

One day . . .
Some dramatic change sets your story in motion. What is it?

_____

_____

_____

_____

_____

Because of that . . . *What happens?*

Because of that . . . *What happens?*

Because of that . . . *What happens?*

Until finally . . .

What happens at the climax—your story's most dramatic point? How does your drama resolve?

And ever since that day . . .

How have your world and your characters changed by the end of the story?

*(If you don't know the answers on this page yet, that's okay!
Write down how you want it to feel.)*

Sample Story Spines

Once upon a time there was a man named Winston Smith. Every day, he went to work for a totalitarian government ruled by Big Brother. One day, he met a rebel. Because of that, they had an affair. Because of that, he read forbidden books. Because of that, he was arrested and tortured. Until finally, he cracked and betrayed his lover. And ever since that day, he said he loved Big Brother.

Once upon a time there was a hobbit. Every day, he lived comfortably in his hobbit-hole. One day, a wizard made him throw a party. Because of that, he heard a story. Because of that, he left on an adventure. (You could fill MANY more pages with "because of that"!) Until finally, he came home again. And ever since that day, he lived comfortably in his hobbit-hole and wrote the story of his life.

Trace the spine of one of your favorite stories below.

Once upon a time there was

Every day,

Because of that,

Until finally,

And ever since that day,

PLOT COASTER

This "roller coaster" is the simplest visualization of a plot spine. But your ideas may take some twists and turns along the way. Mark the basics of your story goals along the curves, then wreck this page by scribbling your own lines and arrows if and when you find your story changing. Use different colors every time you come back.

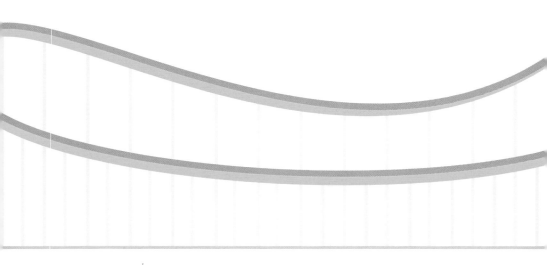

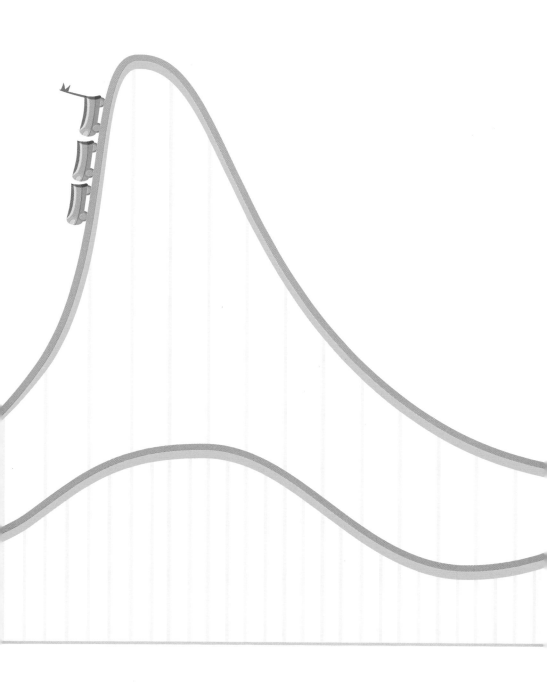

CHOICES & CONSEQUENCES

Every choice, big or small, has an impact. People make decisions rationally, impulsively, out of need, or out of habit. Use the space below to explore choices your characters could make, and the disastrous (or rewarding) effects those decisions may lead to.

CHOICES	CONSEQUENCES
CHARACTER: _____	

CHOICES	CONSEQUENCES
CHARACTER: _____	

CHOICES	CONSEQUENCES

CHARACTER: _____

CHARACTER: _____

CHOICES	CONSEQUENCES
CHARACTER: _____	
CHARACTER: _____	

CHOICES	CONSEQUENCES
CHARACTER: _____	
CHARACTER: _____	

CHOICES	CONSEQUENCES
CHARACTER: _____	
CHARACTER: _____	

CHOICES	CONSEQUENCES

CHARACTER: _____

CHARACTER: _____

CHOICES	CONSEQUENCES
CHARACTER: _____	
CHARACTER: _____	

NARRATIVE BEATS

THE OPENING

Use these flowcharts to help brainstorm your novel's key events and turning points. Work in whatever order feels right to you, and don't be afraid to change, add to, or ditch it later if the story tells you to.

We begin with....

A PERSON: _____	A PLACE: _____	AN EVENT: _____
Who does/is doing...	We see	This affects the world because
Who acts like/is thinking...	We hear	People respond by

PROTAGONIST(S)' CURRENT SITUATION

I hope the reader feels

They feel

PREPARATION AND
CONFRONTATION

We begin with....

A PROBLEM:
....

Who/what is responsible

What is at stake

A PLACE:
....

We see

It's important because

A PERSON:
....

Who is doing....

Who needs help from...

Who is worried about...

Character(s) must

Or else . . .

CONFRONTATION

RESULT

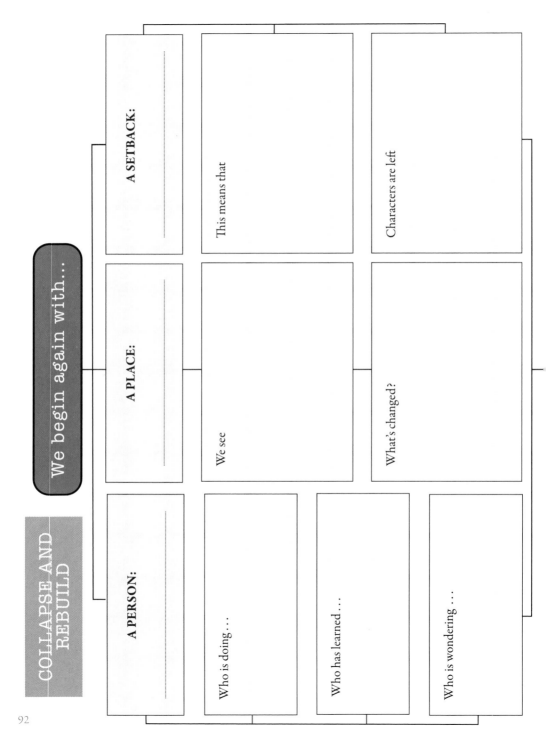

COLLAPSE AND REBUILD

We begin again with....

A PERSON: _____

Who is doing ...

Who has learned ...

Who is wondering ...

A PLACE: _____

We see

What's changed?

A SETBACK: _____

This means that

Characters are left

92

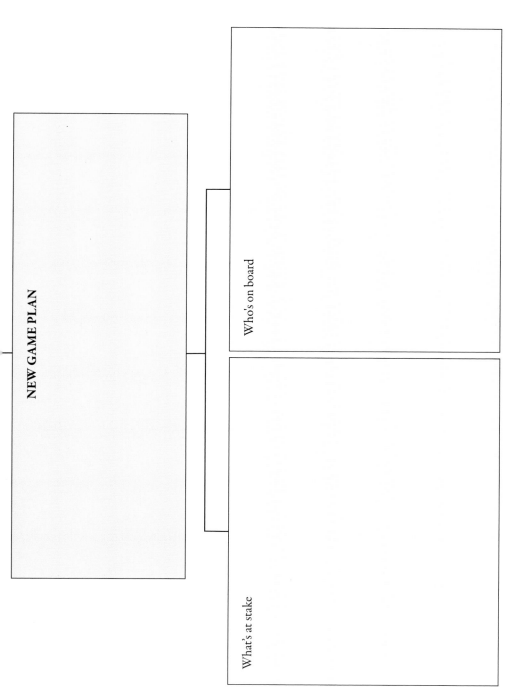

NEW GAME PLAN

Who's on board

What's at stake

93

THE CLIMAX

We begin again with....

A PERSON:

_____

Who is doing....

Who is dealing with ...

Who decides ...

A PLACE:

_____

We see

Why this place? Why now?

A CONFRONTATION:

_____

Confrontations

Circle one or more, or write your own:
Life vs. Death • Life vs. a Fate Worse than Death • Good vs. Evil • Success vs. Failure • Love vs. Hate • Growth vs. Regression • Revolution vs. Stasis

Say more. Why these themes?

Aftermath/Remaining Concerns

What happens?

THE RESOLUTION

We end with....

A COMMITMENT: _____

Things are the same *(for better or worse)*

Things are different *(for better or worse)*

A PLACE: _____

We see

This place is now

A PERSON: _____

Who is doing . . .

Who is feeling . . .

Who is changed . . . .

We're left feeling

We're left wanting

We remember

Conflict is one kind of behavior.
There are others, equally important in
any human life, such as relating,
finding, losing, bearing, discovering,
parting, changing. Change is the universal
aspect of all these sources of story. Story is
something moving, something happening,
something or somebody changing.
— URSULA K. LE GUIN

* * *

SCENE
CREATION

Scene: _scene/chapter name or number_

Situation: _How does the scene begin? Why are the_
character(s) here?

Development/s: _What happens during the scene?_
What does the reader learn? What do the characters
learn?

Outcome: _How does the scene resolve? What_
consequences are set up? What's the takeaway for
the reader?

SETTING

Location: *Where does this scene take place?*

Mood: *What's the tone or "feeling" you want for this scene?*

Environment: *What's here that can help set the tone or advance the plot? (scenery, important objects, weather, time of day/night, etc.)*

CHARACTERS

POV Character:
Who's the point-of-view character in this scene?

Goals: *What does this character want?*

Conflict: *What problem or tension is this character dealing with? How does it put them at odds with other characters, or the overall situation?*

Character:

Goals:

Conflict:
Remember, there are ways to create change without conflict, so fill in these sections with whatever feels appropriate.

Character:

Goals:

Conflict:

Other characters in scene: *Anyone else here? What do they want? Why does their presence matter?*

Last scene: *(page number)* Next scene: *(page number)*

Scene: ....

Situation: ....

....

....

....

....

Development/s: ....

....

....

....

....

....

Outcome: ....

....

....

....

....

....

SETTING

Location: ....

Mood: ....

....

Environment: ....

....

....

CHARACTERS

POV Character:	Character:	Character:
Goals:	Goals:	Goals:
Conflict:	Conflict:	Conflict:

Other characters in scene: ....

....

Last scene: _____ Next scene: _____

Scene: ....

Situation: ....

....

....

....

....

....

Development/s: ....

....

....

....

....

....

....

....

Outcome: ....

....

....

....

....

....

....

SETTING

Location: ....

Mood: ....

....

Environment: ....

....

....

CHARACTERS

POV Character:	Character:	Character:
Goals:	Goals:	Goals:
Conflict:	Conflict:	Conflict:

Other characters in scene: ....

....

Last scene: _____   Next scene: _____

Scene:

Situation:

Development/s:

Outcome:

SETTING

Location: ....

Mood: ....

....

Environment: ....

....

....

CHARACTERS

POV Character:	Character:	Character:
Goals:	Goals:	Goals:
Conflict:	Conflict:	Conflict:

Other characters in scene: ....

....

Last scene: _____ Next scene: _____

Scene:

Situation:

_____

_____

_____

_____

_____

Development/s:

_____

_____

_____

_____

_____

_____

_____

Outcome:

_____

_____

_____

_____

_____

_____

SETTING

Location: ....

Mood: ....

....

Environment: ....

....

....

CHARACTERS

POV Character:	Character:	Character:
Goals:	Goals:	Goals:
Conflict:	Conflict:	Conflict:

Other characters in scene: ....

....

Last scene: _____ Next scene: _____

Scene: ....

Situation: ....

....

....

....

....

Development/s: ....

....

....

....

....

....

....

Outcome: ....

....

....

....

....

....

SETTING

Location: ....

Mood:..

....

Environment: ....

....

....

CHARACTERS

POV Character:	Character:	Character:
Goals:	Goals:	Goals:
Conflict:	Conflict:	Conflict:

Other characters in scene: ....

....

Last scene: _____ Next scene: _____

Scene:

Situation:

_____

_____

_____

_____

_____

Development/s:

_____

_____

_____

_____

_____

_____

Outcome:

_____

_____

_____

_____

_____

SETTING

Location: ....

Mood: ....

....

Environment: ....

....

....

CHARACTERS

POV Character:	Character:	Character:
_____	_____	_____
_____	_____	_____
Goals:_____	Goals:_____	Goals:_____
_____	_____	_____
Conflict: _____	Conflict: _____	Conflict: _____
_____	_____	_____
_____	_____	_____
_____	_____	_____
_____	_____	_____

Other characters in scene: ....

....

Last scene: _____ Next scene: _____

Scene:

Situation:

Development/s:

Outcome:

SETTING

Location: ....

Mood: ....

....

Environment: ....

....

....

CHARACTERS

POV Character:	Character:	Character:
Goals:	Goals:	Goals:
Conflict:	Conflict:	Conflict:

Other characters in scene: ....

....

Last scene: _____ Next scene: _____

Scene: ....

Situation: ....

....

....

....

....

....

Development/s: ....

....

....

....

....

....

....

....

Outcome: ....

....

....

....

....

....

....

SETTING

Location: ....

Mood:..

....

Environment: ....

....

....

CHARACTERS

POV Character:	Character:	Character:
Goals:	Goals:	Goals:
Conflict:	Conflict:	Conflict:

Other characters in scene: ....

....

Last scene: _____ Next scene: _____

Scene: ....

Situation: ....

....

....

....

....

Development/s: ....

....

....

....

....

....

....

Outcome: ....

....

....

....

....

....

SETTING

Location: ....

Mood: ....

....

Environment: ....

....

....

CHARACTERS

POV Character:	Character:	Character:
Goals:	Goals:	Goals:
Conflict:	Conflict:	Conflict:

Other characters in scene: ....

....

Last scene: _____ Next scene: _____

Scene: ....

Situation: ....

....

....

....

....

Development/s: ....

....

....

....

....

....

Outcome: ....

....

....

....

....

....

SETTING

Location: ....

Mood:...

....

Environment: ....

....

....

CHARACTERS

POV Character:	Character:	Character:
Goals:	Goals:	Goals:
Conflict:	Conflict:	Conflict:

Other characters in scene: ....

....

Last scene: _____ Next scene: _____

Scene:

Situation:

Development/s:

Outcome:

SETTING

Location: ....

Mood: ....

....

Environment: ....

....

....

CHARACTERS

POV Character: Character: Character:

Goals: Goals: Goals:

Conflict: Conflict: Conflict:

Other characters in scene: ....

....

Last scene: _____ Next scene: _____

Scene:

Situation:

Development/s:

Outcome:

SETTING

Location: ....

Mood: ....

....

Environment: ....

....

....

CHARACTERS

POV Character:	Character:	Character:
Goals:	Goals:	Goals:
Conflict:	Conflict:	Conflict:

Other characters in scene: ....

....

Last scene: _____ Next scene: _____

Scene:

Situation:

Development/s:

Outcome:

SETTING

Location: ....

Mood: ....

....

Environment: ....

....

....

CHARACTERS

POV Character:	Character:	Character:
Goals:	Goals:	Goals:
Conflict:	Conflict:	Conflict:

Other characters in scene: ....

....

Last scene: _____ Next scene: _____

Scene: ....

Situation: ....

....

....

....

....

....

Development/s: ....

....

....

....

....

....

....

Outcome: ....

....

....

....

....

....

....

SETTING

Location: ....

Mood: ....

....

Environment: ....

....

....

CHARACTERS

POV Character:	Character:	Character:
Goals:	Goals:	Goals:
Conflict:	Conflict:	Conflict:

Other characters in scene: ....

....

Last scene: _____ Next scene: _____

Scene:

Situation:

Development/s:

Outcome:

SETTING

Location: ....

Mood: ....

....

Environment: ....

....

....

CHARACTERS

POV Character:	Character:	Character:
Goals:	Goals:	Goals:
Conflict:	Conflict:	Conflict:

Other characters in scene: ....

....

Last scene: _____ Next scene: _____

Scene: ....

Situation: ....

....

....

....

....

Development/s: ....

....

....

....

....

....

....

Outcome: ....

....

....

....

....

....

SETTING

Location: ....

Mood: ....

....

Environment: ....

....

....

CHARACTERS

POV Character:

....

....

Goals: ....

....

Conflict: ....

....

....

....

....

Character:

....

....

Goals: ....

....

Conflict: ....

....

....

....

....

Character:

....

....

Goals: ....

....

Conflict: ....

....

....

....

....

Other characters in scene: ....

....

Last scene: _____ Next scene: _____

Scene: ....

Situation: ....

....

....

....

....

....

Development/s: ....

....

....

....

....

....

....

Outcome: ....

....

....

....

....

....

SETTING

Location: ....

Mood: ....

....

Environment: ....

....

....

CHARACTERS

POV Character:	Character:	Character:
Goals:	Goals:	Goals:
Conflict:	Conflict:	Conflict:

Other characters in scene: ....

....

Last scene: _____ Next scene: _____

Scene: ....

Situation: ....

....

....

....

....

....

Development/s: ....

....

....

....

....

....

....

Outcome: ....

....

....

....

....

....

SETTING

Location: ....

Mood: ....

....

Environment: ....

....

....

CHARACTERS

POV Character:	Character:	Character:
Goals:	Goals:	Goals:
Conflict:	Conflict:	Conflict:

Other characters in scene: ....

....

Last scene: _____   Next scene: _____

Scene: ....

Situation: ....

....

....

....

....

Development/s: ....

....

....

....

....

....

....

Outcome: ....

....

....

....

....

....

SETTING

Location: ....

Mood: ....

....

Environment: ....

....

....

CHARACTERS

POV Character:	Character:	Character:
Goals:	Goals:	Goals:
Conflict:	Conflict:	Conflict:

Other characters in scene: ....

....

Last scene: _____ Next scene: _____

Scene:

Situation:

Development/s:

Outcome:

SETTING

Location: ....

Mood: ....

....

Environment: ....

....

....

CHARACTERS

POV Character: _____   Character: _____   Character: _____

_____   _____   _____

_____   _____   _____

Goals: _____   Goals: _____   Goals: _____

_____   _____   _____

Conflict: _____   Conflict: _____   Conflict: _____

_____   _____   _____

_____   _____   _____

_____   _____   _____

_____   _____   _____

_____   _____   _____

Other characters in scene: ....

....

Last scene: _____   Next scene: _____

*Writing begins with forgiveness.
Let go of the shame about how long it's
been since you last wrote, the clenching
fear that you're not a good enough writer,
the doubts over whether or not you can
get it done. . . . Concoct a hot beverage,
play a beautiful song, look inward,
and then begin.*

— DANIEL JOSÉ OLDER

***

CHEERING SECTION

DETECTIVE'S LOG

Life is weird. Boost your fiction with some investigative reporting on the eccentricities around you. Use these pages to keep track of all the strange, meaningful, and ludicrous things that you see and hear in daily life, and come back to them whenever your writing needs a dash of inspiration.

THINGS SEEN	DATE

THINGS OVERHEARD	DATE

MEMORY BANK

What you observe can inspire you, and so can your own life story. Jot down places you've been, dreams you've had, memorable moments, important figures from your past and present, and any other experiences that helped shape who you are.

LOCATIONS	DETAILS	DATE

DREAMS		DATE

MEMORABLE MOMENTS	AGE

PEOPLE	QUALITIES	PHYSICAL DESCRIPTION

INSPIRATION CONSTELLATION

Every writer draws inspiration from what they enjoy. Write (or doodle) the books, movies, TV, music, art, and other media you love below, connect the dots between them, and think about the themes and qualities that mean the most to you. Don't hide the impact they have on your creativity—embrace it!

MY HYPE-UP WRITING PLAYLIST

SONG	ARTIST

WORD ASSOCIATION

It's not just a school-bus game. Novelist Ray Bradbury credited his "best stuff" to this exercise, making lists of nouns to track down themes and images that kept coming back to him.
Write down some words with no order or logic at all. Add to the list however often you want. At any time, pick a word from your list and write about it.

FREE WRITING

TOOT YOUR OWN HORN

Use this space to celebrate yourself—strengths you've noticed, lines you're particularly proud of, goals you've met, and ways your story has surprised you.